*Red Raspberries
in October*

Red Raspberries in October

Prose and Poetry
by

Inge Logenburg Kyler

authorHOUSE®

AuthorHouse™
1663 Liberty Drive
Bloomington, IN 47403
www.authorhouse.com
Phone: 1-800-839-8640

© 2009 Inge Logenburg Kyler. All rights reserved.

No part of this book may be reproduced, stored in a retrieval system, or transmitted by any means without the written permission of the author.

First published by AuthorHouse   11/25/2009

ISBN: 978-1-4490-4714-6 (sc)

Library of Congress Control Number: 2009911817

Printed in the United States of America
Bloomington, Indiana

This book is printed on acid-free paper.

Illustrations by Inge

After the Last Harvest Moon

The soybean field is barren and brown rowed
With water lying in the lower end.
Along the fence edge which was left unmowed,
A flock of red-winged blackbirds sing to send
The very last of summer's song as they
Gather in strength for fall's great southward flight.
The morning sun bursts through to start the day
And heightens golden maples with its light.
The heavy frost that coated fields and fir
Fades quickly as the sky begins to blue
And creeping things that slept begin to stir,
Completing harvest of all that which grew
In June. It is the time before the deep
Of winter solstice and the heavy sleep.

First Prize – Lansing Poetry Club Hildebrand Contest 1995
Second Prize – Poetry Society of Pennsylvania Mariah Quant
Contest – 2006/published in PPS Prize Poems 2006

As Seasons Come and Go

The things we did in youth, do you recall?
The running up and down the hills, hands clutched
Together, Love? Beneath an oak's wide shawl
We kissed, and ran around the trees unrushed
At playing games. In spring the laurel found
Its way into my hair. You put it there,
And, later on, a rose. We were unbound
By time. Life was a giant age to share.
I found a rose between a dusty book
This day, withered and brown. The years have flown,
And gone with them—the laurel by the brook,
Wild hills and how it feels to be wind-blown.
The things we did in youth, do you recall,
The dogwood blossoms? *Oh, but now it's fall.*

Second Prize – Lansing Poetry Contest – 1971
Published in The Evening News, Sault Ste. Marie 1972

Preserved on Paper

They were in a box
Dust covered and forgotten
Until now.
Their fragility outlasting the giver
And receiver.
"Dear Friend,
These are for you."
From woman to woman
The parched paper displayed
A friendship
Preserved now
In a jar among jars,
Old jars,
Canning jars,
In a spiderwebbed cardboard box
In a dark corner of a stone wall
Of an old farmhouse cellar.

Published in Peninsula Poets, PSM
Reprinted from Grit, 1994

Sleeper Sliding Through the City

Silently, we slip through towns and cities
Like trains have ever since day one
When the first track brought the first train,
Only this time, it's me, in Sleeper car No. 631,
Room number B with private bath and sofa
And a bunk that drops down so two people
Can sleep in comfort until the conductor
Picks up speed to make up for lost time
After a careless driver in a white van
Thought he could outrun us, and of course
He couldn't, although he lived
To pay the $1500 fine for delaying
A whole trainload of people for an hour!
We pull into stations that look like twilight zones,
Worn gingerbread and barricaded windows,
Because city fathers think trains aren't important
Anymore. Little do they know, since they only
Drive big cars and vote for road improvements.
We're picking up speed now, trying to make up
For the van crash, and the rock slide
In the Truckee River country. It is night, and
The car is swaying! Partitions are separating
And I can see the couple in the next room,
But don't want to, so quietly I shove partitions
Back in place and plaster my face
Against the window, trying to figure out
Where we are as we speed through another city
Where people wave or look impatient
At this nuisance, this train that silently
Slips through towns and cities
Taking people on journeys as complex
As a crowded train station at 5 o'clock p.m.!

The Pump, Lilacs and Stream

If only they could talk; the lilacs, pump
And stream. But winds blow gingerly and stir
But shadows of a dream. A burned out stump
Partly concealed with brush, remnants of fur,
A nest. Some wild thing had housed itself
Inside the grass choked thick with mustard weed.
The pump is black and stands upon a shelf
Of stone. It stands alone—like fading steed
Of West. Cracked bricks, foundation angled, line
What must have held a house, one day, before
The highway came. Imperial, a sign
Reads STOP, where once a path led to a door.
Hardly do travelers notice, when they pass—
The lilacs, pump, and stream, and wild grass.

*Printed in Americana (tape) by Lansing Community
 College, Lansing, Michigan 1976
Printed in Dreamers Live Forever – 1979 – Lansing
 Poetry Club
Michigan Folktales and Ballads – 2000*

Three Cranes In The Sky

It was a day in March. The air was cold.
The trails we walked were fragile as stained glass
As here and there the river had been bold
To capture trunks of trees and brittle grass.
A glint of sun peered from a north-blown cloud
And brightened up a distant stand of elm.
And then a cracking sound close by and loud
Broadcast that forest gnomes were at the helm!
It was the woodland waking up! The ice
Was breaking loose, while water on the bridge
Forced us to change our route. Winter's cold vice
Was letting go. We walked the meadow ridge,
And then we heard the sound of spring—a cry!
We looked to see three cranes high in the sky.

First prize Lansing Poetry Club Annual Contest 2008

Night Journey

I hear the clock: *tick tock, tick tock, tick tock*
With second of the minutes of the night
And wonder what it is that could unlock
The things that are enveloped from our sight?
The weeks melt into months and then a year
For soon a decade's gone, to disappear
Until a memory brings it back to mind.
Tick tock, tick tock. I'm pulled into night's deep
Where I can soar above a slumbering earth
Or do all sorts of things, and laugh or weep,
Reflecting in abstract the moral worth
But then all vanishes. My clock goes *ding!*
Try as I might, I can't recall a thing!

Second Prize – Dale Guhl Memorial Award
Pennsylvania Poetry Society Prize Poems 2007

A Land of Gold

There is gold within the sunrise
That is brilliant in the dawn,
There is gold within the rainbow
That is high above the lawn.
There is gold within the sunset
As a day falls to a fade.
There is gold within a pumpkin
Underneath its orange charade.
How can I feel poor or saddened
When this gold is mine to claim—
If I dare to feel a lacking,
I have only ME to blame!

Published in American Bard 1962

A Child's Path

What does a child remember?
What will he best recall?
How can I give him gladness
Instead of a life that is dull?
How can I give him sunshine?
How can I keep him warm?
How, when life leads his footsteps
Into a swirling storm?
Will he recall the comfort
Of home, and the happy ride—
A sled in the middle of winter,
The cold of the snow, a chide?
Love will comprise his sunshine,
And Truth may well be his coat.
The storm will just build his courage
While Faith keeps his strength afloat.

*Published in Lansing State Journal,
Lansing, Michigan 1961*

A Search for Blooms One April Day

I hope I never grow too old
To walk the woods on winter-ending days
To seek for blooms when air is cold.

I search for blooms among earth's mold
Of leaves and twigs in woodland maze.
I hope to never grow too old

To prowl among the forest's hold
As a release from winter's plays,
To search for blooms when air is cold.

When Solstice comes with clouds unrolled
And old King Cole peers from the haze,
I hope I never grow too old

And hope that I can be so bold
No matter what lies in life's phase,
To search for blooms when air is cold.

An April day, I'd like to hold
And bask within its welcome rays.
I hope I never grow too old
To search for blooms though air be cold.

*Third Prize – Poetry Society of Michigan Nature Contest
2006/ Peninsula Poets of Michigan 2007*

Survivors

They were before and after
The great mud slide,
Enough of them somehow
Evading the Makel's lance and club
To hide in churning waves
Crashing against Pugent Sound's deep grottos.
We peer over the jagged ledge,
Cape Flattery's plunge could be forever!
> *Seal pups dive and lift their heads.*
> *Who's watching who?*
> *Who is the survivor here?*

Harpooned once by Ozette and Quillayute.
They dodge boats, ships and fishermen
Where black boulders, graffitti scarred
Lionize the western coast.
> *The great whale spouts and disappears.*
> *Is his chance of survival linked with ours?*

High above tree tops, almost out of view
The eagle soars, a puncheon of strength.
> *Do we need to see them*
> *The seal, the whale, the eagle*
> *To ensure our own destiny?*

Published in Charles Warren Stoddard, Bristol Banner Books, Bristol, In 1993

After The Lightning

It was just before the storm
When the lightning was bold
And quick
That I saw these little men,
Brave hunters, in the sky
Chasing the flashes of light
With their arrows ready.
Brave little Bushmen,
What manner of men placed you there
With your apricot bodies gleaning?
Was it our doing? We, the
Civilized, who put you there?
And yet, you who threw
Your hearts out to the stars
Are in the depths of every man.
You, at least, feared not your shadow.
Driven out of the desert
You found your home
In the sky and
In the conscience
Of every soul.

*Published in England's Spring Anthology,
Mitre Press, 1966, Published in American Mosaics
Anthology 1968*

As The Crow Flys

The turnpikes go by way of crow
Across neat farms with tranquil charms.
They split the land. It once was grand.
The barn sits there—with idle care.
The house rests here, the overseer
Must cross the wide where motors ride
To get across; and any loss
Is paid by State (with a debate!)
Farms start anew with work to do
To plant and plow and feed the sow.
But what if when there comes again
Another lane to split the rain—
They raise their hands. Lost are the lands!
For man must drive while he's alive.
  But what of stars, when planes chase cars.
  Can they be split to make roads fit??

Published in Driftwood, Ludington, Michigan 1961

Indian Mill

Wild chestnuts grew in fuzzy clusters
Along the fence row where crow perched and cawed
I listened as I swung on the old grape vine.
The forest held bluebells and violets
And frogs leaped into the creek
Where an old Indian Mill hugged the bank.
It was a good place for mud pies
Chokecherry cake and visions of Indians.

Today's forest holds a Day's Inn
While somewhere, buried far below
Is the old Indian Mill.
A century from now it might be found again
And some other little girl will bake mud pies
Chokecherry cake and have visions of Indians.

First Honorable Mention
Pennsylvania Poetry Society Prize Poems 1986

Note: An old Indian Mill is buried in Wolf Run, PA

Autumn Umbrella

<pre>
                The
             Umbrella
         Sky of yellow spokes is
      Sunning the corn and drying oats.
    Farm combines are shredding tasseled wheat.
    Queen's lace by the wayside, fragrance sweet.
    Like rain clouds, the songbirds gather thick. Their
        Aria's   hint   "Be quick,   be quick. Each
                         June
                         Rose
                         Will
                         Wilt
                         Then
                         Gray
                         From
                         Frost.
                         Each
                         Hope
                         Ever
                         Lost
                         Like
                                   Leaves freed
                                      From yokes."
</pre>

Printed in Hoosier Challenger, IN – 1971

Nothing Is For Certain

It was in the woods I heard it
    when I walked one cloudy day.
It had been a snowless winter;
    now it was a freezing May.
I had looked for springtime flowers,
    all I found were frozen shoots,
And a lack of sun had forecast
    only doom for summer fruits.
Thus it was that when I heard it,
    I was startled at the sound
Of the words that were unusual
    with no one, it seemed, around
For I saw no human lurking
    in the brush or by the tree
But the message was peculiar
    that was offered here so free:
"Nothing is for certain"
    were the raspy words I heard.
"Who is there?" I quickly questioned
    but I saw no man or bird!
Now I'm known to be of brave heart,
    not to scare at suspect things,
But I must admit I quickened
    and I fingered at my rings.
"Who are you?" I asked to nothing
    seeing that the woods were clear.
Once again the words came to me
    to affirm my doubting ear,
"Nothing is for certain!"

(Continued)

(Continued)

Now I turned and looked around.
Only clouds swooped low behind me.
    Only breezes made a sound.
"Why tell me?" I now was shouting.
    Was it jest, or was this real?

What was I to do with something
    so absurd? How should I feel?
I was not someone of substance.
    I held not a known role
In the crowded world of mankind
    where black newsprint took its toll.
"Nothing is for certain!"

    What again? How can this be?
"Who is there? Why should this message
    come again, again to me?
Only rustling of the branches,
    rustling of the last year's leaves,
Rustling of the woodland grasses
    like the tears of one who grieves
For a tear falls not unnoticed,
    it can rustle minute days.
It can fall to be a river,
    it can build up many ways.
Now I hurried in my walking
    'till I reached the pathway's end.
Then I turned and looked behind me
    searching out beyond the bend,

(Continued)

(Continued)

And I hurried to the doorway
        of my house upon the hill
Where the comfort of belongings
        brought a warmth to ease my chill,
And I slammed the door behind me
        while I pondered of my plight.
Now I could not hear the warnings
        and I locked the deadbolt tight!

Veined Leaves

Discarded leaves of summer make a pretty face
Scattered in grass just mowed. Frail, vintage lace,
Almost unnoticed as a lakeshore's far flung sands
Yet beautiful with etched design, just like old hands.

Published in Gaylord Area Council for the Art's brochure
Poetry Contest 2008

Orange Alert

Flapping like wings
of those free moving creatures
that migrate north
just because something in them
tells them to, orange banners,
twenty-three miles of them
on seven thousand
and five hundred gates
in Central Park greeted anyone
and everyone
who passed through
mundane February
in the year two thousand and five
because Christo and Jeanne-Claude
spend their lives
making the impossible
possible.

The Phantom Swing On The Walnut Tree

Just a few gray shacks and a lilac bush
And a tree that's gnarled and old.
There's a rusty hoe and a closed up well
And some boards covered with mold.
In the evening time when the dew is wet
Then a song falls from the tree
In the stirring grass, you can hear the words
Singing, "Daddy, please swing me."

Printed in Capper's 1999

Articles selected from many published over many years in the Eaton Rapids *Flashes* Newspaper:

End of a Season

On Christmas Day, like so many families, we gathered together for dinner and friendship. But the day was different from other Christmas days as this time a number of people gathered to play video games in front of the wide tv screen that graces so many homes today instead of watching football games and such. As the afternoon progressed, the conversations became more specialized, specialized, that is, in the area of electronics, leaving some of us in the dark!

"Do you feel overwhelmed?" asked my grandson's wife. I had to admit that I did. For many years I prided myself in being knowledgeable on gadgets such as fax machines and/or the computer. But all of a sudden the world of technology blossomed so dramatically that suddenly I found myself feeling like I was in the dark ages. Maybe this is how my grandmother felt when the world of autos, electricity, and telephones developed! How does one ever keep up?

I decided that it was easy to keep up if you had a child in school. Even my young granddaughter has a cell phone and music recording devices. A young niece has her own web site. But the granddaughter lives in Philadelphia and the niece lives in Washington DC! No help there!

But while they were in town, one of the nieces tried to engage me in computer games. Now I have always pooh pawed games feeling they were a waste of time, especially since I have a hard time getting things done as it is. But little Linda insisted that I play a computer game of ping pong with her, which I did. Wow! This was no easy thing!

(Continued)

(Continued)

Playing the game meant being alert enough to work one's fingers on the keyboard while watching the action on the screen and making the appropriate very quick moves. Needless to say, I need a lot of practice. Maybe playing games is not all that bad after all! "Well," said my niece, "the author of the Harry Potter books plays computer games."

So that has become part of my New Year's Resolutions: to try to educate myself on computer games, gadgets, web sites and such. That is, if I can find a good instructor! This brought another discussion where I mentioned that why is it that the computer gadget stores do not hold instruction classes for those of us who are in the dark in the matter of electronics? Just think of the sales they would make! Maybe that will be another mission for 2008—to find "gadget" instructors. After all, not all of us have grandchildren around to help! *2008*

Black Is the Barn

Black is the barn
  Against red sky
And one bright star
  Suspended high
While trees whose leaves
  Are sparse and thin
Reach for the morning
  Coming in.

Printed in Capper's 1993
Printed in Peninsula Poets 1994

Returning Spring

It's that frantic time of year once again, the time when wildflowers come and go just like that. I noticed that especially with the fragile little bloodroots. I kept watching for them and didn't see them, and then suddenly there they were, but the next day I looked and they were gone.

Spring is like that. I suppose that's why it's called "spring," because everything springs up and then disappears before you know it. My little wildflower patch is burgeoning with mayflowers. I pulled a bunch out so that the trillium could see the sun. The daffodils that were so abundant are now done, and I was able to get out and deadhead them before we left for out of town.

It's the time when things like hosta, need to be divided, but it is hard to find time to do everything. The rhubarb is already up and threatening to go to seed even though all I have harvested so far was enough for a rhubarb crisp. I had hoped to put some in the freezer. Meanwhile, the asparagus is having a tough time. Mother Nature, it seems, is very fickle. She coaxes things to bloom and then zaps them with her freezer wand. Now that I found out how good asparagus is with just a bit of dressing on it, I hope I will be able to harvest some! I also found a good baked casserole recipe.

Most of the little trees we planted out front did not make it through the winter. Even the lilac by the road, looks like Old Man Winter was in a vengeance and killed it before leaving. Well, I did the only thing that made sense: I planted hostas along the fencerow where the trees were. I guess it makes sense to plant things that you know will grow no matter what. I told My Better Half not to cut down the brush that grows along the east side as we need all the volunteers we can get.

(Continued)

(Continued)

Anything I pay a lot of money for, does not seem to survive, so I may as well give in, give up, and let Mother Nature have her way! The barn swallows flew in this week and already are busy setting up housekeeping. The first of May brings in the wrens. Mrs. Wren moved into the gourd birdhouse the day we hung it up! I am now busy preparing some others for occupancy, but if I don't hurry, it will be too late.

So much to do and not enough time to do it all. Well, I guess the best thing to do is to grab a cup of coffee and a cookie and just sit on the porch and enjoy the show. After all, this is what we have been waiting all winter for.
2007

Christmas

It seems to me that the days just go by faster and faster each year and so many things go unnoticed in our busy travels here and there. With the holiday decorations in ample review, it seems I must try to pay better attention to the streets I drive down in order to properly "see" the many displays. Some are cascades of icicle lights and some are blinking blue or fencerows of green and red. There are colorful trees, reindeer, carolers, nativity scenes and then there are the neighborhoods where neighbors seem to be intentionally vying for the biggest display! There are also plays, displays and pageants galore that I would like to see and hear, but there is never enough time to do everything. Like in Alice in Wonderland, who has the time to do it all?

Before we know it, the season is gone and we are putting things away again.

(Continued)

(Continued)

I think back of Christmases past and how it was in our little bungalow down in the valley. Christmas meant my dad taking me to the department store so we could go up to the fifth floor and view the wide array of toys. Toys were not displayed all year like they are today, and because of that reason parents often did not buy toys until the Christmas season. I also remember peeking under the bed one year and found a big mail order box with a doll that had a bruised cheek. It looked like Mom had put rouge on the bruise to make it look better. I hurriedly put the lid back on and got out of Mom's bedroom before I was found out.

Maybe that's why I enjoy volunteering at the State Historical Museum of Michigan. It's almost as if everything there has a life of its own or a memory that comes flooding down. The little theatre with its velvet curtains reminds me of the immaculate theatres in our little town and of the two ladies who took care of it, making sure no one brought anything to eat to their seats.

The dime store display reminds me of the stores where I did all my Christmas shopping, not that I did much as no one had a lot of money when I was growing up.

I think back of the tree my Dad decorated with glow in the dark stars to surprise my Mom and I when we returned home from a few days away to visit her mother. I can even vaguely recall the snap on candles Mom put on the tree branches when I was very small. Most of all I remember that aunts and uncles that would come by or we would drive to visit them. There was such a sense of family back then. It was a real treat when one or two of our glamorous aunts would visit us from Chicago.

(Continued)

(Continued)

Their spike heels, fancy veiled hats and red fingernail polish always enthralled me. Mom would pull out the daybed for them to sleep on.

But memories are built today, too, by the holiday visits and dinners that some of us hold for our own families. We don't know what our own younger family members will retain in their own memories. It might be just a special dish we prepare, like the traditional potato pudding I make every holiday. My grandson doesn't let me forget it, although I almost did at Thanksgiving time! I guess that's what memories are made of.
2007

Searching for Things When Coal Was King

Over steep mountain roads and rocky creeks
Past black-eyed Susan's and pink Jo Pye weed,
Past Anne's Lace and woodlands full of leeks
And cattails swelling brown, bursting with seed,
We drove searching familiar sights and scene
But could not find the house my aunt lived in,
A stucco house with snowball bushes, green
And thick around the porch and coal chute bin.
We could not even find the road. A sign
Faded, peered from the bend. "On Strike," it read.
A tipple loomed beside a vacant mine.
We passed a creek of sulfur rocks ahead.
Stores boarded up told of another day
When coal trucks heaped and rumbling passed this way.

Small Accomplishments:

As I look around and notice there are some gardens that are truly beautiful, I can't help but wonder how people do it? No matter how much I weed and hoe, it seems like a hopeless job indeed, for my own plot.

Of course I blame it some on Mother Nature who makes it too hot to work out in gardens, plus the fact that I have been rolling out of bed later than I should. So I can think of lots of excuses for it's unkempt condition. One of the excuses is that here it is August and before too long the summer will be over anyway, so what does it matter how the garden looks?

So excuses can be the heat of the summer, the dry spells, too many other things to do, or total avoidance due to the overwhelming nature of things and a lack of energy to do them all! Anyway, already the katydids are hollering in the evenings along with the grass crickets. The owl hoots in the waxing of the moon, and the coyotes remind me at nighttime that not all things sleep; all signs of a summer that never lasts long enough.

So what does one do? I guess it is a matter of enjoying each gift of a day for what it is. As I pull a bunch of beets or harvest a tomato, I feel grateful for that special opportunity. It is a good feeling to open the freezer and see the bags of frozen beans, cherries, berries, peas, and such. I know that when the snow flies, all those goodies will be especially appreciated.

There is a feeling of accomplishment when I view the many jars of bread and butter pickles. We don't eat that many any more but other family members remind me that they look forward to them. How wonderful the house smells with the aroma of pickle spices in the works while canning. There are other

(Continued)

(Continued)

special gifts, such as a granddaughter from out of state asking for a second piece of pie from the wild raspberries I had harvested along the fencerow last month!

I guess that's what summer is all about. We do what we can, when we can. The garden may not look as nice as I would like it to, but I remind myself that other things are just as important as spending time weeding. Sitting under a tree and reading a good book while the sun is welcome and warm, is one of them. Baking a pie for someone special is another one. What more can one want?
2006

Light for an Evening Walk

Blue splashed chicory's sea of petals
Laps the roadside by the nettles;
While Queen Anne's lace dressed in white
Shines; a beacon in the night!

Peninsula Poets, 2003

Peace May Come, Someday

Through much thought and much pondering
I wondered of it all.
How could I love my country
When it seemed that it might fall?
So much wrong and such grieving
I thought my heart would bleed.
How could I love my country
When it never hears my need?

So I gathered all my things
And thought that I would go.
The perfect place eluded me
I pondered friend and foe,
Then conceded that this land
Has much that, yet, is good,
So I'll stay and help it grow
And work for brotherhood.
Now I know each country has
Both good and evil, too.
But I know each land depends
On what you and I can do.
I will sing of praises, light
Some candles on the way
And hope for peace and freedom
For every man, someday.
Refrain: A Nation needs its people,
   Needs people everywhere
   So let us join together
   And tell the world we care.

First Prize: Edna Groff Diehl Memorial Award
Pennsylvania Poetry Society 1972
Printed in Prize Poems, PPS 1972

How Wolf Run" Got Its Name

Down around the Susquehanna, where it weaves
    and where it bends,
where the railroad finds a tunnel through the
    mountain's swooping ends,
in the valley where the creeks pour, where
    the hemlock dips and sways,
lived a rugged pioneer couple, different,
    even for those days.
He was rough, and rude, yet friendly. She* was tall
    and dressed the sport
sheathed with knife, and hunting leather, she
    was ruthless in her court.
As she hunted deer and pheasant, other game,
    throughout the wood,
she became a known legend , for her hunting
    was that good!
Then it was, she bagged a creature, that to all,
    was quite a prize,
and her mate, who rowed to meet her,
    saw the wolf she bagged; its size
was like nothing ever captured, and when all
    was said and done
that the creek, where she had bagged it, from then on
    was called "Wolf Run."

*Near Clearfield, Pennsylvania
*Mrs. John Carothers, circa 1802

A Chicken Story

In days of trials and tribulations, it seems right to have a chicken story! Why chickens? I just can't help but notice that chickens seem to be the funniest creatures around!

On my way home while driving down M-99, there were two red windblown chickens, pecking along the road, unconcerned of the 60 mph traffic whizzing by. They instantly made me think of fried chicken, and I wondered if they would survive the day!

Emily, our one and only hen, is a good case in point. She and Elmer were a team, until Elmer, that is, bit the dust. We weren't sure what happened, except one morning there he was, laid out for all to see, and as dead as a door nail!

Emily didn't seem too bothered about his demise. In fact, the way she was cackling and faking crows, we weren't sure she wasn't singing, "He Made Me Do It!" If you haven't seen the movie "Chicago," you wouldn't understand!

Elmer was buried in the chicken yard, complete with a sign: "Here lies Elmer. He was a good rooster." When I went outside soon after, it looked like Emily was trying to dig him up. Was she filled with remorse? Who knows!

One thing for sure, Emily has a temper. Since we have a number of coyotes prowling around, we close Emily in at nighttime. Emily anxiously waits for someone to come and open the door. She doesn't stand back, however, and wait until it's opened. Rather, she kicks it open with a big huff as if to say, "What took you so long" as soon as the latch is pulled.

(Continued)

(Continued)

When we are outdoors, she hurries to the fence and begins her chattering. Yes, chickens have their very own chatter! If only we knew what she was trying to say!

After Elmer died, we heard a strange noise that sounded like crowing.It was Emily! Did she think she had to copycat Elmer now that he was gone? Even though she is alone, she seems content. Maybe she likes it that way. We could get a few more chickens so she would have company. However, chickens have a sociability problem in that they rarely like other chickens, not unlike some people in the world!

One thing for sure, Emily faithfully presents us with an egg almost every day!
2003

Muddy Rivulets

Muddy rivulets
Stream beside the road
Sun dissolving winter snow.

Woods Runner, Sault Ste. Marie, MI 1987

Lady In Black

From another era
she yet wears black:
a black veil; shading old eyes
and worn lids.
Regal in bearing
she stands tall and erect
her feet shod
in black sturdy shoes
over black stockings.
Wearing a black dress
she carries a heavy
black purse
as if she is still in mourning
for a partner
gone now thirty years,
and just maybe any other color
might cause him to rise
from the grave
and just maybe
she is happy
the way things are!

Gaylord Arts Council Prize Poems 2008

For Fragile Things Lost

Minnie may never again be the same,
Her head just a little misshapen
From the glue, but, too,
Neither will Mickey, who fared far worse,
Losing both his head and an arm, as well.
Three green crystal dessert tumblers survived,
Three more did not,
And only one blue porcelain egg cup
Endured Humpty Dumpty's fall.
The plate from Alaska survived,
Albeit two chips that maybe
Can be sandpapered and smoothed out,
And miraculously two platters from Sturbridge
Are still intact.
The mug from a German cousin
Many years ago, is shattered,
As his marriage turned out to be,
And the little dishes from my childhood
Or maybe my daughter's,
There seems to be some debate whose they were,
Are gone but for the little tea and creamer stamped
"Made in Japan."
Somehow, the mandolin, on the floor below,
Survived with only a broken bridge,
But the prized cranberry glass vase,
Placed innocently beside the mandolin,
And filled with silk flowers, did not,
For it was a mighty crash
That hot humid 90° July day
That stirred us all
The day the catwalk
Left the wall.

Thoughts At an Old Cemetery

Even though I was on the edge of my seat,
Watching the roadway, we missed it,
Until suddenly out of the corner of my eye
There was a concrete pillar
Barely visible on the steep bank.
"That's it!" I said as we edged the van
to park along the dirt road.
We disembarked to explore what was left
Of the old church grounds
Where grandma and grandpa
And some of their friends were buried
In the weed chocked old German cemetery.
I hadn't remembered the hill
Being so steep before, and wondered
How people must have labored
Carrying beloved to this resting place.
Tumbled down pillars led to the front
Of what was left of St. Paul Lutheran Church.
Nothing there now except a gaping hole
And rocks. I tried to imagine
How mother, as a young woman,
Must have looked when dad,
On his first visit stepped off the train
From the tracks across the road.
He had just come from Germany,
A handsome man, twenty year or so old.
All the girls had their eyes on him,
But my mom said, "I got him!"

Peninsula Poets 2001

A Jacket Story

In looking back, I hate to see the old year go. It was a year of tumult events from watching as life long friends suddenly succumb, sons and daughters going off to war in a far off land, watching as beloved family members succumb, and, on the home front, watching as beloved animals succumb. In the later, it was our golden Lab in August, and then our elderly cat that fell over and died suddenly, from an apparent stroke, just last week.

How does one cope? Well, one looks back and tries to find the good and, yes, the humor, in all of that. The good was the fact that, in the case of loved ones, we were lucky to have known those beautiful people, and in the case of the animals, we were lucky to have owned them for the time that we did.

In the case of the war, it prompted us to travel again to California to visit with family while our son was in between going back and forth to the Mid East. We had a great visit and some wonderful memories. We might not have taken the trip out, had it not been for the uncertainty of the times. Then, the humor of things; with all of the funerals going on, some of them necessitating us packing and unpacking our bags and traveling distances, we did not, until this week, realize that sometime in the summer, the suit jackets of my husband and his brother-in-law, got mixed up when we stayed with them for a few days. I wondered, when I started packing for a funeral, why the jacket and pants seemed to be off color. Maybe it was the lighting, I decided, and dismissed my doubts while frantically finishing up the packing.

I should have been alerted when my spouse announced that he must have forgotten to snip the pockets open on the jacket, this being said while we were on the way into the funeral parlor. Did no one notice that the suits on both men, each wearing the other's jacket, were off color? Apparently not! So much for

(Continued)

(Continued)

detail! After we got home, we received a long distance call that asked that we look at our jacket. Sure enough, it was quite apparent that the jacket we had in our closet was not the one that went with the pants. It was also obvious that the mistake was made at an August funeral and went undetected during the November one, as well! This gave us all quite a number of laughs. It released the tension of a stressful and somewhat sad year!

Note: After this article was published in *Flashes,* the postman delivered a package and said: "I"ll bet this is your jacket!" It made us all stop to think that a year is how you view it in the end. In the end, it was a good year, after all. It also told me that the local postman reads my articles! *2004*

> Cold wind that's gusting through the tree,
> Has missed the flock just taken flight.
> Gray clouds are all that one can see.
> Winter descended overnight.
> *Third Prize – Lotus Knowlton Roberts*
> *Memorial Contest*
> *Pennsylvania Poetry Society Prize Poems 2007*

An Old Shed

What is it about an old shed
an old gray shed
leaning precipitously
like a monk
kneeling at the alter
in prayer, perhaps,
for dignity
and painless wearing down
in the passing of the years.
Both limited in ways
to mark the days;
the monk in his platitude to God
the shed,
in its beams grinding to sod.

Peninsula Poets, Spring 2009

Flight of the Nez Perce

When winds are quiet one can almost hear
Soft whispered anguished pleas among the fir;
The cries of sorrowed people as they flee
Across cold barren rock and rough terrain
Endless plain and sagebrush hills
Between tall rugged mountains, stark, snow-capped
Across rivers that held glints of gold
They hurried following the raven's cry
They hurried feeling their pursuer's drive
Their hearts were sorrow-laden filled with fear
At what may lie ahead and everything familiar
Left behind.
Driven like cattle into snow, the old
The babies, no one left the trail.
Hungry, cold and ragged, yet they ran
Thinking that surely peace lay just ahead.
It was not to be.
Among the dead, dying and defeated
Chief Joseph stood in truce.
His people and their dreams scattered
In the wind that drove them and yet
He stood, saying he "would not fight again
For evermore."

Printed in Midwest Poetry Festival brochure 1987

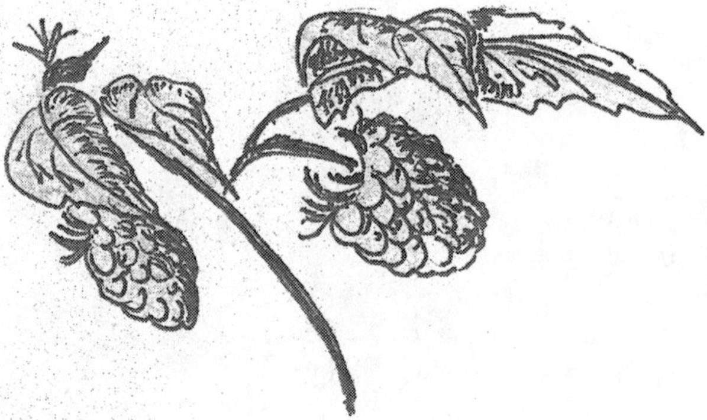

How To Find Martha's Pancake Place

Go six blocks north past Franklin's Bar
Past Tony's Store and Bill's Used Car,
Past mattresses on sale by Dan
Past Kenny's Tires, and Susie's Tan
Past Carla's Hair, and Nails by Jill
And Henry's Service down the hill,
Rebecca's Childcare, Lou's Antique
Paul's Swimming Pools, Sarah's Boutique,
Chimneys by David, Homes by Wayne,
Septic by Larry, Tiles by Blaine,
Kayaks by Steven, Art by Glenn
Gardens by Heidi, Books by Gwen.
Then go for just a block or so
When you smell pancakes, well, you'll know!

When Clearfield Became a Town

In the beginning, it was fields and hills,
Chinklacamoose, where Indian families lived,
and hunted until lands across the sea
brought white settlers who would come to claim
the land as theirs, and deals were made.
Formed March 26, 1804, the county of Clearfield
sought land for its local government
when Albert Witmer in 1812
offered "Prime land for any town along
the bank," meaning the Susquehanna, of course,
and thus the town was created, buildings built,
streets laid out, a school, jail, tannery and mill
came to be, and by 1836 its citizenry
boasted three hundred! Three taverns sprung,
hotels and all those things people want
for growth and activity. Logging, rafts,
mills, with people coming and going
with later years bringing brickyards, railroads,
and coal mines.

Today, the Native Americans are gone,
as are the industries of old
including the teeming brickyards
and the comings and goings
of big steam engine trains that wound
through tunnels and steep bridges;
and gone are the black coal dusted tipple miners
and the men who worked the railroads
every day. Pictures of days gone by
are housed in a museum. People come and go
and the Susquehanna River still rolls along
in the Allegheny Mountain valley.

Black Boots

They were out of style
Zip up black galoshes
Placed far back in the closet
Off season, but it was winter
And I reached for them,
Pulling them, one at a time
On the fidgety feet
As the owner held on to chair arms
While I tugged and pulled
Until finally
They were on.
I tried not to think back
When those feet were seldom still.
"There you go, Mom."
She looked and smiled
While placing a booted foot
In front, one at a time
With her ninety-two-year old hand
Firmly on mine.

Second Prize, Jack Gillespie Memorial Award
Pennsylvania Poetry Society Prize Poems 2007

She Was Josephine

Ever summer morning
she opened the front door
letting the sun stream in, and on the porch
after straightening pillows on the swing,
she sat down to admire the morning glories
that were stretching to the rafters
and peering in the windows
where she had just hung paper drapes
in a house that was as cozy and neat
as she was, despite five children
and one on the way.

She was Josephine
married to a terrific cook
who worked at Charle's Bar
and drove the oil truck
to the coal strippings.
He was round faced and jolly
when the bottle was set aside.
Josephine knew his weakness
but she also knew his strength
which was kindness
and a loving heart
in a life in the Allegheny Mountains.

She was Josephine,

What Would Mother Say?

What would mother say
If she could see it all now,
The Old Place, that poor little bungalow
Trapped in the middle
Of an industrial district,
An area Mom and I both knew
As green and forested, wild-flowered,
Visited by the wild deer, the black bear,
The red fox with the clear Wolf Run creek
Letting us splash and play.

It was not that way anymore!
The stream is orange from strip mining
And the mountain where we picked berries
Roars with semi after semi
Racing each other on Route 80.
The only wild life remaining
Are the drunks and prostitutes
That weave in and out
Of that sad little bungalow
That my dad had built so long ago
With his own hands.

What would mother say?

On Dad's Birthday

It is July 23, and would have been
Dad's birthday, had he not died
At 56 so long ago.
When we visit the mountains
Of my childhood
I think of Dad and those fantastic dahlias
And old fashioned roses
That he tended faithfully.
And I recall our picnics
On the big rock in Lick Run
Now inaccessible
Due to a million plus dollar bridge
Spanning high above
That steep winding curve
We all loved,
And I wonder,
Do tadpoles still play there
In the creek,
On this, dad's birthday?

The Dentist

"Doesn't it make you feel bad,"
Asked my family dentist when I couldn't reply,
My 9-year-old mouth crammed
With the buzzing smoking drill
In the pre-Novacane days
"that your sister should be so beautiful
While you.."and then he stopped
But I knew what he meant
And I also knew
There was nothing I could do
About Fate.
My sister and I were like that,
She was "Rag Mop" and saxophone
While I was ballet and violin.

We divided the bedroom, the bed,
And the closet that we shared.
She was my older sister,
Yes, beautiful with blond hair
And blue eyes of the same robin egg blue
Of my handsome dad.
She liked to party, beer, and boys
And couldn't understand how I
Could latch onto just one
And stay with him forever!
I never forgot the dentist's words,
But I consoled myself, as years went by,
Knowing I had one thing
My sister did not:
Naturally curly hair!

The Day I Grew Up

I still remember that day
When I first saw him. He was seventeen,
Puffing on a cigarette
With other boys his age
And something about him
Caught my eye, and at fifteen,
I suddenly realized
There was more to life than ballet, 4-H,
Or writing poems. Here was an opposite
That I had never explored,
An identity that I had never known.

Girlfriends had helped me take down
The Grange booth. It was a girl thing
But when we walked that eight miles,
That August, after we left the fairgrounds,
And reached that swimming hole
Down in the laurel strewn mountains,
And we suddenly came upon
Those five boys,
Girlhood disappeared
Into womanhood.

Red Raspberries In October

It was like finding gold
that unexpected, for the dog and I
were seeking a Christmas tree,
for the holidays.
We had prodded through dry weeds,
stiff goldenrod and tall grass,
barbed briars and thick brush
gnarled vines and old trees
until suddenly I found one,
two, then more
red plump raspberries
growing along an abandoned fence
in a forlorn corner
of the pasture.
Picking them one by one
I let the red juice slide down my throat
marveling how a land
could hold secrets and surprises
for so long and wondered
how many nice surprises there are
in life if only
we take time to look.

       Sledding on the road
       Freed by winter's blustery winds
       Go August corn shocks.
       Printed in The Lookout – Lansing Community College,
       Lansing, Michigan 1993

A Boyhood Remembrance

"It was the weekend and I got to stay
Down in the valley in the old homestead
Where dogwood petals draped the woods in May
And cherry blossoms showed their tinge of red.
The Susquehanna lapped the violet field
Where Whip-poor-wills called with a haunting tune.
The great and graying barn would often yield
A place for scampering on hay in June.
Yet even this secluded place held fear
For in another land a war was on
That seemed to touch our valley, even here.
I felt the seriousness one early dawn
When I spied, where the mountain's train tracks run,
My uncle, by the tunnel, with a gun." *

*As told by Arthur J. Kyler

First prize – Col. Shoemaker Memorial Contest
    Pennsylvania Poetry Society 1987
    Published in PPS Prize Poems 1987
    Published in Peninsula Poets of Michigan 1994

Company Town, Revloc

It was in the '40's
That we drove an hour or more
Up and down mountains
Stopping along the way on a grassy knoll
For a picnic or for Dad to search the trunk
For the kit needed for tire repair,
Or in the middle of a snowstorm
When the click click click
Meant a chain repair, right there
And then we stopped along the road,
While my sister and I read
Funny papers from the Sunday news
To keep us distracted
On the bumpy ride, but we knew
When we were close to my uncle's house
For we could smell the bony pile.
That smoky, acrid, putrid smoldering pile
Of shale that led or turned away
Anyone coming or going, until there we were
In a town where all the houses looked alike
Gray, two storied, family structures
Lined up on gravely roads.
"Company towns," they were called,
And when we visited,
We could hear voices on the opposite wall.
Without fail, after we left,
Dad would remark, "how can they stand
To live there in those look-alike houses
With paper thin walls
And smell those bony piles every day?"

(Continued)

(Continued)

But we all knew
Even young as I was back then
That coal companies and bony piles
Meant food on the table.
  Third Prize – Colonel Henry W. Shoemaker
  Pennsylvania Poetry Society 2006
  Published in Prize Poems 2006 - PPS

Mountain Laurel in June

In the mountains and the vales of Pennsylvania
When the springtime is about to slip away
Then the woods are white with blooms of Mountain Laurel
And the night becomes almost as bright as day.

Mother Carey as the ultimate designer
Scatters petals in the woodlands newly green
So that every laurel bush is bright and shining
And the mountains are a flowered dazzling scene.

Where Lilacs Yet Bloom

Along the Susquehanna, lilacs grow
Beside the road that skirts around the riverbank
Lush purple blossoms bloom and nod as if to show
That long ago it was their role to flank
The barn, the farmhouse and the milking cows.
In memory I yet recall those days
When every field was tilled, busy with plows
And woodland paths wound over hills a ways.

The Interstate changed that, and need for coal
Meant stripping verdant land.
Coal mining chewed the lands and draglines stole
The laurel and the hemlock trees. The stain
Of orange shale stayed. Above the highway roar
My thoughts float back to all those days before.

Published in Poetry Society of Michigan Peninsula Poets 2008

The Ashram

To the mansion of the most ornate
 Go men who seek to know
To dwell among the jewels of souls
Left there so long ago.
Soft glorioles of hidden stars
Dance through wide doors of brass
Mysterious doors that weigh of iron
 And yet shatter like glass.
The morning star appears in view
 No breath is felt or heard
The world of wisdom users through
With advent of one *word*.
There is a knock. Then gongs and chimes
Create a hallowed din.
The yogi bows in acquiescence
 In the ashram of within.

*First prize in Mary McClellan Lyric Contest,
Lansing Poetry Club, 1965
Published in Defiance College Journal 1967*

Poems from "The Wind and the Wood", New Athenaeum Press, FL 1961

Wind and the Wood

The wind and the wood on the mountain's steep slope,
The wild old grape vine that is taut as dried rope
All beckoned and called for me hither to come
To listen to rushing of streams' gentle hum,
The squawking of crow and the woodpeckers' drum—
But I couldn't heed the bold call to come!

I felt that the tree with the dogwood so white,
The rustling of willows in deep of the night
Were whispering, echoing for me to see,
Were swaying and bending down only for me
But I, in my heart, knew I could never be
Now lured from the city, the wood to see.

The lovely pink laurel were blooming so true.
The sky o'er the hill was a brilliant bright blue,
But I couldn't go, for I had here to stay.
A prisoner in city walls for today.
Yet, oh, how I longed for to see the grass play!
But I couldn't go, for I had to stay.
The valley beside the steep rolling green hill,
Was dressed now with daisies that never were still!
The fern by the thick marshy bank that I knew
Would shine like gold stars with the morning's fresh dew
And hold a sweet peach that was ever so new
But I couldn't leave, certain, this I knew.
Oh, wind and the wood, may you not fade away
For I will be back there again some far day

(Continued)

(Continued)

To listen to crickets beneath each tall tree
To wade through the stream that flows swiftly and free
To pluck at the laurel that blossoms so white
And then I will sleep when the darkness brings night.

The Tale of Ravenwood

Ravanwood, Ravanwood
There's the call of Ravanwood!
Echo thru the glen, echo thru the wood!
Pioneer dreams and Ravanwood.
In fall's first frosty misty day
I found my love beside a bay.
I found her perched near cabin small;
She was so fair and sat so tall.
Her hair was long and black as night.
My heart thumped wildly at this sight.
And then a call went thru the vale—
Ravanwood, Ravanwood.

So glad was I to know her name
I knew I'd never feel the same,
My eye felt stayed upon her hair
And on her skin so wondrous fair.
Her head was down, bent on the task
Of kneading a small colored flask.
I knew at once my life was made for—
Ravanwood, Ravanwood.
Then rising from a rough hewn boat,
Her father came in deerskin coat.

(Continued)

(Continued: Ravanwood)

He looked so stooped and worn with age
Just like a favorite book's old page.
He bent to pat his daughter's hair,
And then I wished that I could dare
To touch that shining sheen of black.
Ravanwood, Ravanwood.

I could not hide for long behind
That arching tree that was so kind
With shaking knee I dared to meet
This pioneer creature, virtue sweet.
I felt not like a man of strength
But like a boy with legs of length,
And certainly felt shy and sorry.
Ravanwood, Ravanwood.

Her eyes raised up to meet my own.
They had a gleam that shone and shone;
And I a vowel tried vain to speak
It issued forth—a vague word's squeak.
Then we both smiled. The shell had broke.
(Would this be gone when I awoke?)
T's not a dream that harbors me, but—
Ravanwood, Ravanwood.
Beneath the thick wood's sheltering pine
I courted her and claimed her mine;
And week by week I'd wander there
To watch her work or stroke her hair.
No toil could slack my constant power

(Continued)

(Continued)

That sprang in me from that first hour!
And nothing did I fear or dread since—
Ravanwood, Ravanwood.

The moons flew fast, and fall was o'er.
The hint of winter's snow did soar.
And then one last October day,
I wed this girl from Greenwood Bay,
While overhead the sun shone down
The last time on her velvet crown,
And then I kissed her gentle lips—
Ravanwood, Ravanwood.

Then, from the night's bold darkened hand
I heard a drum of marching band
Beat thru the trees that men bent down.
I knew a curse had struck the ground.
A courier rushed thru country vale—
Now war had come with whirlwind gale!

Come fight the British! Fight the British!
Ravanwood, Ravanwood.

I'm not a man to e'er stand by
And let the other fellow die.
I know what's right; I know what's wrong.
A battle's horrid,--freedom's strong.
While thoughts pressed on my worried brain
Of instant death or months of pain,

(Continued)

(Continued)

I took my leave of—
Ravanwood, Ravanwood

The sun sulked near a grayblack cloud
As tho' it were not very proud
That man should take arms 'gainst another,
And fight his own God-given brother.
But courage won, I raised my pack.
Shouldered my musket, then glanced back
To see my lovely wife—
Ravanwood, Ravanwood.

No, war is not a place of love.
The heavens opened up above.
The armies were soon soaked with rain.
Brown mud clung like a sick man's pain!

As if we were all cursed with sin,
But love of home kept strength within,
For naught can stay a worthy cause.
Ravanwood, Ravanwood
The roads were endless, forests thick.
We marched forever; men were sick
Struck down with Small Pox, still endured
To cross the turgid waters, ford.
They slept some nights in blankets wet
From nightly storms, but didn't fret.
For even a sick man knows his strength.
Ravanwood, Ravanwood.

(Continued)

(Continued)

Each man had visions in his mind
Of all the loved ones left behind;
And I was surely not alone
As thoughts engulfed me of my home,
And weeks turned into months of war
Made ravaged land a blighted sore.
Destruction, ruin were everyhere.
Ravanwood, Ravanwood.

Old cloth took place of shoes long lost.
While rubbish 'round each camp was tossed.
And men now lean from lack of food
Could only stare about and brood.
In ragged breeches, torn old coat,
Small wonder questions struck a note
And men deserted shamelessly.
Ravanwood, Ravanwood.
I forged the streams that told of danger
Pulled up bateau with rank or stranger
Then to retreat from roaring gun!
Back down the stream from pounding drum!
The wind grew strong with cold that sank
Its icy fingers in each rank.
But, yet the battle of time pursued!
Ravanwood, Ravanwood.

And so the years were quickly spent.
Burgoyne surrendered, lives were bent
From loss of friend and shattered wood.
But man with pride did what he should—

(Continued)

(Continued)

He marched for home where every dream
Would somehow show a battle scene.
Amazed that he was still alive.
Ravanwood, Ravanwood.

I started down the woods and path
I had commenced before in wrath
And now a little older grown
I hastened quickly for my home,
While thinking of my treasure there
That deemed to give me further care.
And I should see again my—
Ravanwood, Ravanwood.

Then down the bend and past each tree
The smell of pine felt good to me.
With lightened heart and love-filled mind
I left all thought of war behind.
Because of love that stirred me on
I did endure a challenge strong.
For life survives thru war and loss.
Ravanwood, Ravanwood.

Mining Town

Sprawled over the hills like soft thistle down
Slept little neat homes, here and there a town
Whose future and hopes relied on the ground
That underneath dwelled a treasure mound,
Where tipples and shafts led the way through earth
And finding success, a new mine gave birth
To thousands of tons of a stuff jet black
Assured food and clothing on each person's back.
At four or at five in the early dawn
Dim lights in each home soon would flicker on.
Aroma of coffee then caught the breeze
And mingled with eggs and a slice of cheese.
The men all arose and consumed their fare
And smelled a quick whiff of the mountain air.
They dressed all in black or in navy blue
And reached for their hard helmets, carbon, too.
They checked through each box of red dynamite
Beneath the pale shadows of morning light.
They said their goodbyes and went on their way
While dreading that they mightn't return today.
For who can predict avalanche of rock
Or bear up the brunt of a brutal shock—

A mine that has caved in and filled with gas.
Disaster beneath the green growing grass!
A miner's a man of determined skill.
A man of a trade that's to tame the hill.
And never a flaunt of a college degree
Belittles a miner in history.
For much intellect and a conquered skill
Demands a keen wit to thus mine the hill;

(Continued)

(Continued)

And many a man with a different aim
Caught in the Depression, claimed mining fame.
On now to the mines they went on their way
Descending down winding roads, banks of clay
Past piles of dark shale to the tipple's head
Each coal truck there waited with empty bed
And cars stood stark grim on a crisscross track
Just waiting to glide through the mountain's crack.
The men went to each appointed place
Began the exertion of daily race
To swing hard the pick while the salty sweat
Soaked into each shirt until wringing wet!
And faces once clean now were smudged with soot
And red mucky clay stuck to each dark boot.

The faint fluttering lights on the helmets shed
Their rays down upon the dark tunnel's head,
Directed the way for a pick to fall
That echoed and banged its rough labored call.
The cars stood in line 'till they all were full.
The miners then gave all their strength to pull
Until each car slid down the twisting track.
They roared and they clanged out the mountain's crack!
Then up to the tipple where scales could tell
That everyone finished their day's work well.
Then down to the bed of the truck below
Coal fell in fast heaps like a darkened snow.

The loaded trucks went with their cargo to
The trains standing by for their jobs to do.

(Continued)

(Continued)

The coal went onwards for a way to find
A deed to partake down the mountain wind
In cities, close homes for their warmth or chore
Or else to aid Pittsburgh's hot iron ore.
Then when suppertime said the day was done
The miners emerged from the tunnel run
With empty lunch bucket clasped in an arm,
They gratefully went to their homes' clean charm.

They peeled off their blackened clothes, and they then
Bathed long 'till each felt like a man again.
The sun and the dew held a special place
For each one who toiled with a darkened face.
They sank in their beds very glad for the rest
Until the next day's grueling sweaty test.
A town, though, can lose all its pride and cheer
Whenever a mine is closed year by year.

The people all seek and the people ask—
Where now can we go to find us a task?
Then food is soon scarce and the clothing's gone
And no one knows how or where they belong
And then they must face to a hidden fear—
The whole town itself may soon disappear.
A mother's who's donned in an aproned dress
Will secretly cry of this awful mess
For now she must watch her sons move away
To seek a city with work and pay.
The men walk the streets to discuss their woe—
The end has now come to a life they know!

(Continued)

(Continued)

They feel no great love to a diesel train,
Or a furnace of oil or a high airplane
For they know these things, somehow made them poor
So that they are miners, for nevermore.

Hillbilly

Hillbilly Bill and sweet ridgerunner Sue
Lived in the toe of the mountain's dark shoe.
Dwelled in a shack that was brown and too small
Tucked in the woods where the gay bluejays call.
Hitched one spring day by the Justice of Peace,
Bill took a bath and wore pants with a crease.
Sue wore her dress from a pink flowered sack
Then they retired to their home in the shack.
Lived by the plow and raised number of kin—
Kin who were little and seemingly thin
Coming quite fast, but they raised them quite good
Scolded them like any smart parent should.
Sent them to learn in a school on the hill
Boasting one room that was easy to fill.
Kids stayed at home if a chore needed done.
Sometimes they hid and played hooky for fun.
Then if they luckily reached the eighth grade
Quit! For they thought that they "had life made."
Life in the mountains was quiet and calm.
Man held his life in a big calloused palm.

(Continued)

(Continued)

Tax men could never get out quite that far
Rutted bad roads well could ruin a car!
"Tators they raised on an acre or two.
Stored them in the earth when the season was through.
Money, they earned from the ripe timberwood
Else sold for junk an old rusty car hood.
Once in a month they went in town to buy
Vittles or beer just to make their time fly.
Cared 'bout no dress or tailored man's suit.
Purchased a gun so at crows they could shoot.
Bought a meal sack with a pretty gay print.
Topped with a bag crammed with red peppermint.
Ambled on home in their ancient jalop'
Cardboard for windows, a dingy old top.
Finally got home late Saturday night.
Woods then were dark but the high moon was bright.
Settled on back to live best way they could
Living a life that they thought was real good.
Never did vote, and they never did care.
No politician could find them out there!
Never saw cities or cared thus to see
Sidewalks of concrete or ships on the sea!
Never did care 'bout a distant far land.
Never cared folks lived in styles much more grand.
No care for china, they clung to a jug.
Never saw turnpikes, an airport or tug!
Never did care and they never did see
Zoos, or museums or parks that were free.
Couldn't believe of a different way
Other than living each same old day.

(Continued)

(Continued)

Never did harm, for they lived very good.
Kind hearted folks in the neck of the wood,
Knew of a Black Book that spoke of His Word.
Feared of a Hell, some strange place they oft' heard,
Nevertheless they remained in the hill—
Far as I know, they are living there still.

The Wind and the Willow: A Ballad

The wind on the edge of the pine and the willow
Was touching, caressing and smoothing my brow.
Oh, wind on the edge of the pine and the willow,
Somehow I can still feel your tenderness now.

I long to go and seek once more, away from city wall,
To feel the wind's sweet, fresh embrace,
And listen to its call, listen to its call.
I told you my dreams and each hopeful desire,
I told you my sorrows and pangs of despair.
You nourished my hopes with a kindly indulgence,
Dispersed all my woes with a soft tranquil air.
Now I am where there are no pines. No willow
  Would belong!
But I forever hear the rustle
Of the wind's soft song, of the wind's cool song.

Printed in Scimitar and Song magazine, 1961
Printed in The Wind and the Willow brochure

Susanna's Shoe Ballad

Atop the rolling mountain where pink laurel lines the shore
The river laps the years along, erasing things before.
You may just find an old tin cup, a rusty nail or two,
And maybe, if you're lucky, you will find Susanna's shoe.

Oh, there's nothing remaining now, the farmhouses are gone,
And a factory is rising on old Susanna's lawn!

Tangy lemonade was served with strawberry shortcake,
And lots of other kinds of food heaped on each person's plate,
Folks sang and laughed the time away above the tunneled track.
The Susquehanna rolled along, and night was cool and black.
Oh, there's nothing remaining now, the farmhouses are gone,
And a factory has settled on old Susanna's lawn!

The mountains surely hide within their witness of those years,
The birthday cake so greeted with Susanna's joy and tears.
She kicked her shoe, the fiddle struck, and dancing would begin.
She didn't care what grandma thought might be an awful sin!
Oh, there's nothing remaining now, the farmhouses are gone,
And a factory is smoking on old Susanna's lawn!

Printed in *Down In the Valley* Poems 1980

Our Town Has Spoken

If a town could speak, what would it say
of things that come and go away,
that time of nothingness and then
a blacksmith shop, a 5 & 10,
a school, a church, a roadway there
and needs that take a special care.

If a town could speak, what might it tell
of citizens who know so well
of things a council must address,
monies to raise, lands to assess,
of councilmen who burn the light
attending meetings day and night.

If a town has pride, and well it might
for those have special foresight,
for those since 1842
and onward saw a vision through…
in 1996 today,
if our town could speak—what would it say?

Perhaps a town can speak, has spoken
as here we see a pledge unbroken,
our people built a new Town Hall.
Perhaps towns do speak, after all.

Written and read for Delhi Charter Township's Open House, Holt, Michigan 1996

Articles from *Flashes*, Eaton Rapids Newspaper:

The Banjo: *Summer 2007*

Our California son mentioned that a piece of his luggage was missing when he came home for a recent vacation. I thought nothing of it as luggage often turns up missing when we travel by airlines, but it always pops up. So far, anyway. It was later that I found out that the missing luggage was Grandma's banjo.

When I was growing up in the Pennsylvania mountains, my Dad would get out his banjo and strum it from time to time. His favorite song was: "When I was single, my pockets would jingle, I wish I was single again!" No one during those years had much change to make pockets jingle whether a person was single or not. But the song was cute and obviously I still remember it.

After we moved to Michigan, Dad's banjo could not be found. Its departure has always been a mystery. I doubt that Mom would have sold it while Dad was working out of state, but then I was never sure. However, it was Mom who was the true natural born musician. Today when I hear of people who are older and say they want to learn a musical instrument but are "too old", I think of Mom. She never let age get in the way of anything she wanted to do.

Already a very gifted pianist, once we got settled in Michigan, she tackled the accordion and became proficient at it. By then she was in her fifties, and was proud that she could hang out that coveted sign: "Music Lessons." But not until she was in her early eighties did she decide to buy a banjo and start taking lessons. Maybe she remembered Dad's banjo although both his banjo and Dad, had been deceased for forty years! By the time Mom was in her late eighties, the banjo was too bulky for her small frame to handle, so we went to the music store

(Continued)

(Continued)

and bought a smaller sized one. While at the store, Mom's cane became missing. When I looked around at all the wooden handles of instruments, I felt the cane would be lost forever, but, no, someone found it and brought it to her.

Music was on her mind until at age ninety-two, the celestial musicians needed some instruction and she dutifully went. Just the day before, she had asked about the whereabouts of her accordion! I was left with a ton of music of all kinds, an accordion, and two different sized banjos. I sold the smaller one but kept the other.

All of Mom's grandkids were music gifted. I was not surprised when our youngest son elected to add the banjo to his wide musical instrument collection. But apparently the brothers, this past year, had discussed the banjo and our Williamston son decided he would like to try his hand at it.

Wouldn't you know that the airlines misplaced, of all things, the banjo! Where did it go? I thought of that banjo going to California and back at least twice. It finally did return to Michigan. But in thinking about it, I realized that Grandma lives on through her music! She would be pleased to know that her legacy of a love of music yet survives. She would get a big laugh about her traveling banjo! It's a pleasant feeling knowing that memories of Grandma still survive. Now I suppose I should do something about the accordion still in my closet.
Flashes: Summer 2007

Time for Skiing

With signs of winter ending, I almost (almost!) already miss the skiing around the trails. Recently while skiing there were so many interesting things to see. By a grove of fir trees I spotted a "snow angel" made by a hawk. Of course it wasn't playing in the snow, for a small hole nearby was the clue that Mr. Hawk was after the country mouse. It looked like he probably got it.

Further down around the trees were the heavy trails of the eight deer that routinely crossed our backfield. Here and there they had laid down or stopped to explore this or that. There were highways of little tracks. I tried to figure out what they were. On down the field I was able to ski across areas that soon would be completely flooded with water. What fun it was to scoot under bushes and briar to reach places usually inaccessible after winter. I seriously thought of digging out my old ice skates when I saw the clear patches of ice.

Skiing, however, was much more fun. I kept on towards the pines. I didn't hear the owls that were hooting just a few days ago. There were several calling to each other from the tops of the fir trees. The crows were antagonizing them which got me thinking of the days when there used to be bounties on crows. It didn't seem fair, to see these hordes of black crows picking on these magnificent wood creatures. I thought of learning how to target practice and maybe bag some of them. But the thought only lasted until the next day when the crows and the owls both disappeared.

I sat down by the big oak, my skis strategically pushed under the bench and just sat there awhile absorbing the sun. It was then that I saw a shiny brown creature sliding down out of a small maple tree and then scurrying down through the brush. It must have been a mink! When I went home I looked through my book of mammals and, yes, it had to

(Continued)

(Continued)

have been a mink. The tracks matched the little tracks I had seen earlier. That solved that mystery.

I will miss the mystery of the snow tracks. The brush in the woods is starting to redden and some birds have already started their spring songs. As much as I enjoy skiing, I look forward to the walks through the grasses and meadow when they are green again and filled with the creatures of the meadow.
    February 2008

> Lone morning sunbeam
>   penetrates the east barn wall
>   to glisten star-like

Third Prize – Haiku Award
Pennsylvania Poetry Society Prize Poems 2001

Visit From an Angel

While the weather was still pleasant, I decided it was a good time to look over storage things in the loft over the old garage. Things stored up there include college papers, letters, and such, which belong to the children. No one has had time to go over them and discard unwanted things. So of course Mom and Dad get stuck with things like that.

The boxes had been up there over ten years and were starting to show their age. It was also quite apparent that visitors had been frequenting the loft quite regularly! When I opened the tattered box of science projects, several little "scientists" immediately jumped out! Of course I jumped, too! My Better Half to the rescue, carried the box down the rickety stairs, mice jumping out as he carried it! Whew!

This meant a trip to the store for mousetraps and mothballs! After I repacked a number of things, and discarded a number of things, it got me in the mood for going through old photos that were stored elsewhere. This was a major endeavor! How could we possibly have four large cartons of photo albums? But as I started going through pictures of trips taken and family members here and there, it got me to thinking. For instance, I still think it was an angel that approached us on a trail we were hiking in California in September!

There we were, going down, down, down on a hot 94-degree day, not to mention high altitude, on our way to see the Feather Falls. The sign had read 3.5 miles one-way. I didn't think that would be a problem as we had been hiking and walking regularly. But as we descended into the valley, I began to worry that I might not be able to climb back out of there!

(Continued)

(Continued)

By the time we had reached 3 miles, I was worn. My feet were okay, encased in the hiking boots we had brought with us on the train, but my body, as a whole, was exhausted from the heat. I told our son to go ahead but that I would stay behind and he could see the falls on his own.

It was then that a lone hiker appeared from nowhere, stood there awhile watching us, and then casually mentioned that he was returning via a 4.5 mile hike out of the canyon that was downhill and over a few streams. Downhill? I knew I could do the extra mile! I hadn't realized there was another route!

Thus refreshed, I finished the hike, climbing over rocks the rest of the way to the falls. They were spectacular as they were one of the largest falls in the United States. I had made it. Later, the map read "9 miles." I had done it! I looked at the pictures and thought about the "angel." Who knows?

November 2003

Never Enough Time

How can it be that it is already July? Yet, although it seems that summer barely began, things are already moving much too fast. All winter I looked forward to the lupines to bloom in the herb garden, but when they did, the weather was so wet and cold that I barely enjoyed them, and now they are gone.

The whole month of June, it seems, was a total washout. The good thing about June is that other than one lonely June bug that was banging against the screen door one day, there have been few bugs. Last year it seemed I couldn't keep them out of the kitchen.

The birds have been in a frenzy coaxing their young out of their nests. The first batch of barn swallows has taken flight. We watched their exodus as one by one they tried their wings.

A second batch of young squirrels have claimed the back yard, running fearlessly up and down the feeders and the hemlock tree. A batch of young raccoons was discovered under the hay in the barn. After they were discovered, their mother quickly moved them during the night. However, big grandfather raccoon has been bending over the bird feeders and trampling over new bushes and plants.

The little dog has been getting little sleep at night, being on guard duty at the windows all night long. Little does he know that he would be no match for a big raccoon! The strawberry patch redeemed itself and yielded a crop that more than met my expectations. With guilt for its reward, each day I try to pull out a few more weeds until now it looks almost decent.

(Continued)

(Continued)

The onion crop looks promising, as do the potatoes. But we're not out of the woods yet. A planter that looked so beautiful one day was suddenly attacked by something that next day left nothing but spindly stalks.

A fence was placed around the peppers, peas and lettuce to keep out the rabbits. A trip to the store provided defense against the crawly predators that seem to rise out of the soil as soon as something tasty and green appears.

July seems to evoke memories of family picnics long ago when families gathered and drove to the parks for watermelon and pie. I think of Mother's fine cream pies that were usually pudding by the time we got to the park, but that was the way I liked them. It's a wonder she got the pies there at all, as refrigeration and coolers as we know them today, were unknown.

I miss the family gatherings of those days. Now our small family is scattered far and wide. There is yet the County Fair to look forward to, however, and with that, I guess that is what summer is all about—remembering summers of old and enjoying summer today, whatever it may be.
2005

Unwelcome Visitor

March blew in with hellos to the new and goodbyes to the old, at least that's how it seems to be. As the red winged blackbirds came soaring in and lilting their happy songs, so the little Dark-eyed Junco quietly took off and headed for its breeding grounds up north. How quickly things change! One morning the feeders are full of Juncos and the next morning they are gone. Just like that.

The longest of winters is finally starting to wind down. Or at least that is the hope. This past week found us checking the bluebird houses and cleaning them for their new occupants. Ten houses were cleaned and made ready. Four houses along the east fence row were left for the deer mice. It seemed reasonable, seeing that several were thus so occupied. One family was unceremoniously dumped when it was not realized until too late that the next was occupied. The startled mouse went scooting along the brush probably disgruntled that it would have to rebuild.

Evenings have been honored with the hoot of the owls. Once in awhile one ends up outside the bedroom window. Of course days and evenings are also filled with other sounds and smells, some not so pleasant, like the skunk that ventured under the front porch and ended up fighting with the opossum that had already dug a hole and taken up residence. Needless to say, the encounter resulted in that familiar horrible smell that wafted through the entire house from upstairs to downstairs. It also resulted in the downfall of both animals, not to mention the trouble and work of crawling under the porch and then fortifying the outside against further intrusion. We like our wild animals but we like them better when they stay down in the woods or along the fence row. When they venture up to the house and start causing trouble, then it is time to consider terminating the friendships.

(Continued)

(Continued)

Our Williamston son found out, also, the hard way that being friends with the wild is not a mutual friendship. When pine squirrels start chewing into one's house, chewing through walls and roofs, then it is time for warfare.

I suppose this is a time to enjoy the quiet or, I should say, freedom from invasion of the insect kingdom. Every once in awhile a beetle or fly is seen on the windowsill, a dim forecast of what is yet to come. As I begin the annual cleaning of cupboards and drawers, I try not to forget that plastic bags and containers, although a nuisance, are a necessary confinement tool for rice and beans and anything else that a bug might otherwise consider for housing. One has to be ahead of the game.

The little dog and I walked down to the Big Tree, scattering deer here and there and then stopping to watch the little stream that is freeing itself from ice and snow. It is all a wonderment of change. When I returned to the house, I sat with my coffee and brownie awhile in a chair that now is back on the back porch. I know that there may yet be more snow storms to come. But having a day of warmth and sunshine now and then will help to make the wait for spring bearable. Listening to the newly returning spring birds helps, also.

Bubbles

It was an "I Love Lucy" moment in my laundry room. I have to blame it on the detergent industry. For one thing, why is all the detergent now concentrated? Don't they realize how hard it is to break a habit of how much detergent to use for a load of clothes? Not only that, but the choice of detergent is mind-boggling. When I went to the store for a new supply, I found that all my favorite brands now come in concentrated quantity only. Then there is the top loading, front loading, with bleach, without bleach, with scent, without scent...and it goes on and on. It almost takes a rocket scientist to just make the selection. I just wanted a bottle of ordinary detergent so I could do the normal loads of things to wash!

Once I made my selection and tried to control my measuring it into the washer, I was, I thought, being very careful when suddenly the whole container slipped out of my hands and fell into the machine! Now at the price of detergent, I tried my best to scoop out as much as I could! But needless to say, I didn't get it all back in the bottle. Well, I had to do a wash, so I set the controls and went about other duties.

It was later that my husband came in and asked why there was water all over the floor? Sure enough, the laundry room floor was covered with water. Upon inspection, when I opened the lid of the machine, bubbles greeted me. There were bubbles and bubbles and more bubbles! This was bad as it already was into the rinse cycle. By this time, bubbles should have been dissolved. Not so. Due to another problem, my husband had channeled the hose into the laundry tub. It quickly filled with bubbles. I did the only reasonable thing I could think of, which was to scoop up as much of the bubbles as I could and save them for another wash.

(Continued)

(Continued)

I did that, however, after I moped the floor! The little dog that usually sleeps in the laundry room by the washing machine made a quick exit when he saw bubbles on the floor. He didn't want to get blamed for something he didn't do! I thought about the "I Love Lucy" movies I had watched in years past. This was definitely such a moment!

After it was all over, I tried to locate an old bottle from the "days before concentrate" to find out what kind of detergent had I purchased? No such luck! I had removed the label and turned the bottle into a plant watering can! Sometimes you just can't win!

Untrampled Grass by the Old Barn

At first, it seemed the best thing to do,
"Tear it down," I said. "There's quite a demand
For old barn wood." I might just as well
Have said, "Let's sell your tools, or fishing rods,"
The look I got. It's hard to understand
How one can love a barn. The shake roof was starry
With holes left from shingles that took flight in a wind.
One day after a windblown summer storm,
I found some in my carrot patch beside the zinnia row.
A piece of iron rod lay there, too. I thought of danger,
Flying metal from an old barn in a heavy wind,
But I bit my tongue. The main wide sliding door,
If you could call it that, banged this way
And that until it was fastened down.
I hung a grapevine wreath on the big door.
I can see it from my kitchen window.
The sturdy silo blocks the east wind.
Another matter, that silo, and one I cannot discuss.
Floor rafters in the barn seem strong and rugged,
Though spongy in places where rain has soaked.
The grandchildren would swing on the old brown rope
Until I said "It could come down, you know.
Who knows how strong or weak the rod might be?
He said nothing, but I noticed the other day,
It was gone, wrapped around a high beam
Out of reach like the ladders that stretch

(Continued)

(Continued)

To windows facing north and south. Someday,
I'll climb those ladders, maybe, when he's not looking.
He said he does. The barn holds pulleys, bolts, hooks
And rods that only he knows what they are for.

Cobwebs, bird nests and old beams
Fill the basement stalls, while light switches lead to old wire
That drapes precariously to the farmhouse.
I leave the barn, and return to my own domain,
The kitchen, to finish my pie baking
Using the pink rhubarb that someone else planted,
While I ponder this old barn that stands so lonely.
Before I went to bed, a last look at the pies
Lined on the kitchen counter, made me notice a ray
Of moonbeam skimming across the floor.
Looking out the window I saw a golden round moon
Suspended in fast moving clouds illuminating
The barn with shimmering moonlight,
It was then that I understood.

Two Goldenrod Poems:

I.   Painting Goldenrod

How can I paint goldenrod
when I see your agony?
How can I smile
when I feel your pain?
The world's vastness
exposes everything
to everyone
that pain like osmosis
seeps into the very being
and doing
of everyone
everywhere,
and if it is comforting to know,
others do cry
others do feel pain
others do feel anguish
but I will continue to paint
goldenrod
and the purple wild aster
because in so doing
I am part of the wind
that touches everything.

II.   **Goldenrod**

The goldenrod is blooming in the field
like springtime dandelion, its golden head,
and yet it is not hope for things to come
but things that were; a period to reflect
that catches in my soul like water pools
along a sandy road. The nights are cold
when just awhile ago I could not catch
my breath but for the fan that stirred and cooled
the humid air. The swallow family soars
around the barn, it's summer nesting place,
as if to strengthen wings for that long flight
to journey with the clouds that overnight
blew from the north. The clouds hang low
and soar like skiers over hills and towns
blowing the doors and windows shut, forcing
each living thing to scurry in its haste
to put away, close up, make ready for
the unknown tempest of a winter's cold.
The bittersweet has yet to bloom, its bud
tight as a nut before it cracks the pod.
The katydids have done their song, and gone
just like blue chicory that brightened roads,
their lacy heads of white now turned to brown
and curled like bird nests that still cling to trees.
The cold air stings and tears are quick to come.
We are chameleons in a world of change.

(Continued)

(Continued)

as if to cushion unseen things or threats
that could impede the busy going here
and there. The moon is halved but for a night
yet seen through eyes across the world's vast globe
and seems as tempting as an orange half peeled.
The goldenrod is blooming in the field.

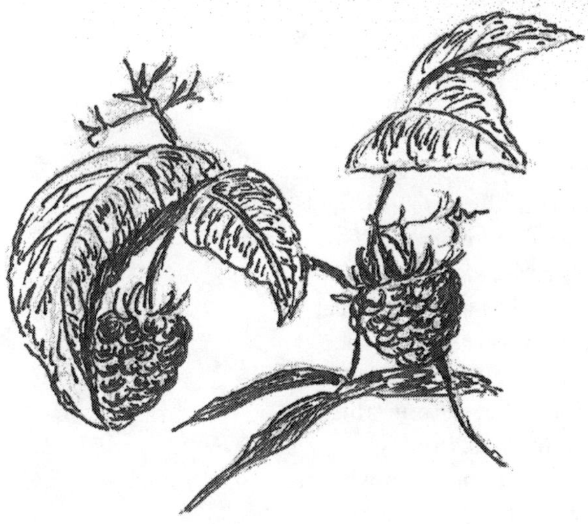

Visions of the Far East

Wrapped in tissue, dates and figs
Lumped the red felt stocking
Draped lovingly over white-tissue
Wrapped presents, gifts from my Dad
Under "my" side of the tree.
While tasting those Far East delicacies
I savored every bite
Imaging rubies, emeralds,
Camels and drifting sands
With three Wise Men traveling
To find a Babe.
Today at Christmastime
I purchase dates and figs
Although my Dad is gone,
My own children are grown
But the rubies, emeralds,
Camels and drifting sands
Yet materialize and are as real
To me now as they were then
When I was a little girl
In the Allegheny mountains
Who found dates and figs
Under the tree on wind-whipped
Snowy star-filled December
Christmas nights.

Cappers 1993

The Wedding Dress

In the l950's, it was the norm for girls to marry soon or even during, their high school years. In my case, my wedding was planned for October 30, 1954, the fall after I graduated from J. W. Sexton High School, Lansing, Michigan.

I was to marry my high school sweetheart. I met my husband-to-be following the take down of the 4-H and Grange booths at the Clearfield County Fair, Clearfield, Pennsylvania, where I attended school until June 1953 when my family migrated to Michigan for employment. With two girlfriends, we walked to a swimming hole in Lick Run, which was about an eight mile walk from the fairgrounds. When we got there, four boys were already swimming in the creek. That was the beginning.

When my family migrated to Michigan, my boyfriend and his friend, also migrated for the same reason: work! There was no work in our hometown due to the closure of brickyards, railroad yards, coal mines and all those things connected to those industries.

My family joined the Unity of Greater Lansing Church in the Lansing area. They did not have a church building at the time and met in the YMCA. It was in the YMCA auditorium in which we were married. In those days wedding receptions consisted of light sandwiches, cake and punch. It was a small wedding. My sister, Betty, was matron of honor. My husband's friend, George Collar, was best man. George's brand new wife, Nancy, also stood up for us, as did Bud Otto, a member of the church. About forty people attended our reception after the wedding ceremony performed by Nora S. Hines, the Unity minister.

(Continued)

(Continued)

My parents, William G. and Marie Logenburg, and my husband's parents, Emerson and Josephine Kyler attended our wedding. My gown was purchased from Greens in downtown Lansing on September 4, 1954 for $35. The pioneer beaded hat and veil, which were so beautiful, disappeared during the reception and no one has been able to figure out what happened to it! The wedding party and immediate family went to the County Kitchen in Mason, for a chicken dinner.

Having a very old car, we could only afford to drive to Grand Rapids where we spent the night and the next day window shopping. It started spitting snow and I had no mittens, so we headed back to our new apartment at 1715 ½ Beal Ave., in Lansing, MI. We didn't know if we would be able to afford the rent, even though I was working for the Parks Department of the State of Michigan Conservation Department, as a stenographer. My husband was employed with Boyer and Son as a construction worker. The apartment rent for two little rooms was $14.00 a week. We lived there until the next May when we bought our first little home on Hilliard Road in Lansing, for $7500.00. Our family began with the arrival of Heidi Rose, August 28, 1955, followed by Steven Daniel, April 4, 1960, and Glenn Arthur on August 15, 1963.

We celebrated fifty years of marriage on August 8, 2004, the only date Glenn, a career Air Force Captain, could come in from California with his wife Rebecca. With the War on Terror, he was overseas most of the time. We celebrated with the folk band, The Scarlett Runners, and Sam Herman, a banjo player. On our eighteen acres, we were able to accommodate over a hundred people in our pole barn, barn, and tent in the back yard. Our "fifty" party was a party of fun and joy for family and friends. Cousins came from Cincinnati, Flint, Chicago, Pennsylvania, etc., ..some of which I had never met.

(Continued)

(Continued)

It was a glorious day to celebrate fifty years of togetherness. We had subs catered from Hobie's in Lansing, mini cheesecakes and cream puffs from Sam's Club, and I prepared a wonderful bean salad from a Depression Cook book recipe! Our daughter in law, Becky, took charge of decorating and serving. Our place was decked with barrels and quart jars filled with wildflowers gathered from local fields, gold table coverings, and gold balloons which we released to the sky when the party ended. A neighbor who was a professional photographer offered to take pictures of our family group. He refused payment so I painted a picture, one day, of their backyard pond and wildflowers. They hung it in their livingroom.

And yes, I was still able to fit into my wedding gown which I hung for display! I had forgotten about the gown until my nephew's wife asked me if I still had it, and if so, could she see it. Thus, it went on display. If one looks closely, one can still see the confetti trapped in the bodice of the dress. It is from the shower every bride received after a wedding in the fifties!
Note: I was eighteen and Art was twenty when we were married. The gown is on display in a little museum in St. Johns, Michigan.

Table of Contents   Page

A Boyhood Remembrance 56
A Child's Path 9
After the Last Harvest Moon 1
After The Lightning 12
A Land of Gold 8
An Old Shed 44
A Search for Blooms 10
As Seasons Come and Go 2
As The Crow Flies 13
Autumn Umbrella 15
Black Boots 49
Black Is the Barn 24
Company Town, Revloc 57
Flight of the Nez Perce 45
For Fragile Things Lost 40
Goldenrod 95
How To Find Martha's Pancake Place 47
How Wolf Run" Got Its Name 35
Indian Mill 14
Lady In Black 39
Light for an Evening Walk 33
Mountain Laurel in June 59
Muddy Rivulets 38
Night Journey 7
Nothing Is For Certain 16
On Dad's Birthday 52
Orange Alert 20
Our Town Has Spoken 79
Peace May Come, Someday 34
Poems From the Wind and the Wood: 30
Hillbilly 74
Mining Town 70
The Tale of Ravenwood 64
The Wind and the Willow: A Ballad 77

(Continued)

Title **Page**

Preserved on Paper 3
Red Raspberries In October 55
She Was Josephine. 50
Sleeper Sliding Through the City. 4
Survivors. 11
Susanna's Shoe Ballad 78
The Ashram. 61
The Day I Grew Up. 54
The Dentist. 53
The Phantom Swing On The Walnut Tree. 21
The Pump, Lilacs and Stream 5
Thoughts At an Old Cemetery 41
Three Cranes In The Sky 6
Untrampled Grass by the Old Barn. 92
Wind and the Wood 62
Veined Leaves 19
What Would Mother Say?. 51
When Clearfield Became a Town. 48
Where Lilacs Yet Bloom 60

A few of many Articles Written for *Flashes*, Eaton Rapids, Michigan over twenty years:

Title **Page**

A Chicken Story 36
A Jacket Story 42
Bubbles 90
Christmas. 27
End of a Season. 22
Never Enough Time 86
Returning Spring 25
Small Accomplishments 31

The Banjo 80
Time for Skiing. 82
Unwelcome Visitor: 88
Visit From an Angel 84

The Wedding Dress. 99
Conclusion 107

Conclusion

Many years have passed since I moved from Pennsylvania to Michigan, and although I have come to love my "new" state, especially Lake Michigan, there is always that mystical feeling attributed to one's home town and birthplace. I feel lucky that I grew up in an era when woods and forest covered much of the land. Industrial districts and huge box stores were unknown. It was a time when I could walk over the mountain to visit a girl friend, or could hitch hike to town, without fear.

Yes, there were dangers even in those days. At one time I nearly fell victim to one when a possible child abductor tried to lure me into his car on my mile walk to catch the school bus. But my parents taught me not to be afraid, to use good judgment, and to be alert.

Thus unencumbered by fear I was able to walk the mountains, smell the mountain laurel and swim the cold streams. Those were the days before strip mining for coal came along and ruined many of the little creeks and streams. Those were the days of the sprawling puffing brickyards, and the scene of men working on the railroads nearly every day, and of black coal mining clothes being aired on the clotheslines. I can even remember the days before electricity, when kerosene lamps lit our home and when most women were homemakers. I am glad I lived during those days. I hope that through my poetry, some of those days can be made real for readers.
Inge Logenburg Kyler